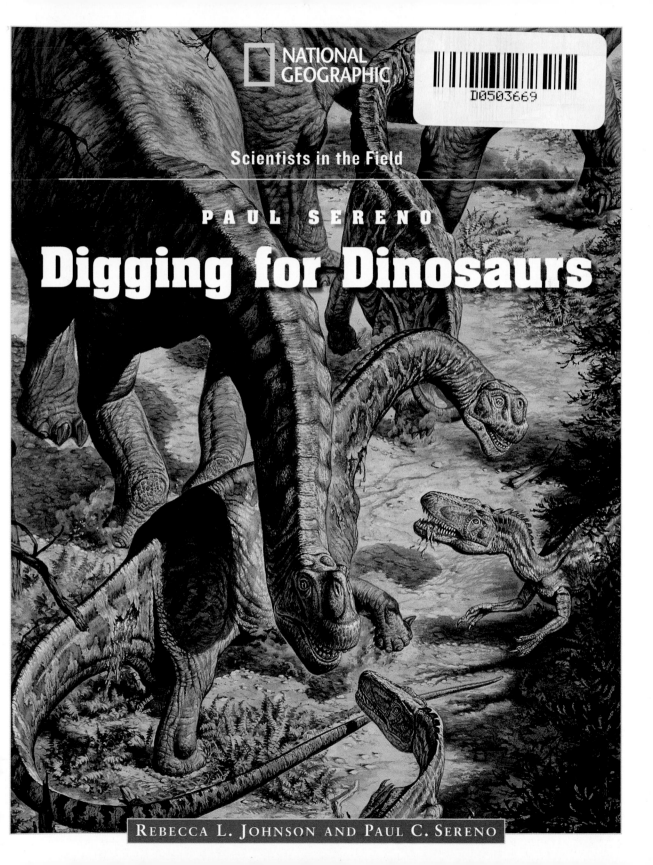

NATIONAL GEOGRAPHIC

Scientists in the Field

PAUL SERENO

Digging for Dinosaurs

D0503669

REBECCA L. JOHNSON AND PAUL C. SERENO

PICTURE CREDITS
Cover: (inset) Mark Thiessen/NGS Image Collection, (background) Hans Larsson.
Pages 1, 27 art by Mark Hallett; pages 2–3, 5 (top), 14, 15, 16 (right), 17, 18, 19 (top), 22, 30, 30–31 (background) © Mike Hettwer, courtesy of Project Exploration; pages 4, 6, 7, 10, 12 © Paul Sereno; page 5 (lower), 16 (left) Equator Graphics; page 8 Neg. no. 318651, photo by Charles H. Coles, courtesy the Library, American Museum of Natural History; page 9 © David Varricchio; page 12 (silhouettes) © Carol Abraczinskas and Paul Sereno; page 13 Dennis Cook/AP; page 19 (lower), 21 (lower-middle) © Burke/Triolo/Brand X Pictures/PictureQuest; page 20 (top), 20–21, 21 (top left) PhotoDisc®; page 20 (lower) © George Steinmetz; page 21 (top right) Forestry Suppliers; page 21 (middle) © Image Source/electraVision/PictureQuest; page 21 (lower right) courtesy of Paul Sereno, photographed by Mark Thiessen; page 23 © Chicago University Hospitals; page 25 Kameno Pajic/AP; page 29 Lloyd Wolf.

Back cover: (top to bottom) Kip F. Evans/NGS, Emory Kristof/NGS Image Collection, Michael Nichols/NGS Image Collection, Johan Reinhard/NGS Image Collection, Mark Thiessen/NGS Image Collection.

Produced through the worldwide resources of the National Geographic Society, John M. Fahey, Jr., President and Chief Executive Officer; Gilbert M. Grosvenor, Chairman of the Board; Nina D. Hoffman, Executive Vice President and President, Books and School Publishing.

PREPARED BY NATIONAL GEOGRAPHIC SCHOOL PUBLISHING
Ericka Markman, Senior Vice President; Steve Mico, Editorial Director; Barbara Seeber, Editorial Manager; Lynda McMurray, Amy Sarver, Project Editors; Roger B. Hirschland, Consulting Editor; Jim Hiscott, Design Manager; Karen Thompson, Art Director; Kristin Hanneman, Illustrations Manager; Diana Bourdrez, Tom DiGiovanni, Ruth Goldberg, Photo Editors; Christine Higgins, Photo Coordinator; Matt Wascavage, Manager of Publishing Services; Sean Philpotts, Production Manager.

Production: Clifton M. Brown III, Manufacturing and Quality Control.

PROGRAM DEVELOPMENT
Kate Boehm Jerome

BOOK DESIGN
3r1 Group

Published by the National Geographic Society
Washington, D.C. 20036-4688

Product No. 4J41283

ISBN-13: 978-0-7922-8887-9
ISBN-10: 0-7922-8887-4

Printed in the United States of America

4 5 6 7 8 9 10 11 19 18 17 16 15 14 13

Cover photo: A crew member, on a Sereno expedition in the Sahara, unearths *Jobaria* bones.

The team for the Niger 2000 Expedition poses for a field portrait in the Sahara.

CONTENTS

Piecing Together the Past

Towering rock formations in the Ischigualasto Valley, graveyard of the dinosaurs

Paul Sereno picked his way down a rocky slope. Out of the corner of his eye, he spotted an odd-shaped stone. No, not a stone—a bone! There was another bone next to the first, and another. Paul had found his first dinosaur skeleton!

Paul Sereno, paleontologist

In 1988 Paul and a student team traveled to the Ischigualasto Valley in Argentina. The oldest dinosaurs, legend had it, were to be found in this desert valley. There, some 40 years ago, scientists had unearthed bones of an early dinosaur they called *Herrerasaurus*. But no skull or complete skeleton had been found.

Herrerasaurus lived about 228 million years ago when dinosaurs were first appearing. Over millions of years, dinosaurs spread across the globe. They **evolved**, or changed over time, into thousands of different **species**. The last of the dinosaurs died out, or became **extinct**, about 65 million years ago.

But dinosaurs left clues. Footprints, bones, and teeth were preserved as **fossils**. These are the kinds of clues Paul Sereno examines as he explores the past. So get ready to join Paul Sereno, world-famous dinosaur detective, as he pieces together the story of dinosaurs.

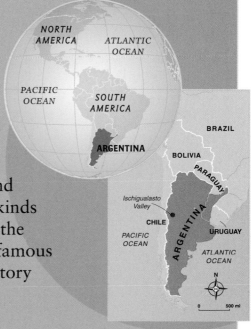

CHAPTER ONE

Paul Sereno
Painter to Paleontologist

Are you crazy about dinosaurs? Can you rattle off dinosaur names from Apatosaurus *to* Velociraptor? *Believe it or not, Paul Sereno hardly gave a hoot about dinosaurs at your age.*

Paul Sereno grew up in Naperville, Illinois, a suburb of Chicago. His mother was an artist and a teacher. His father was a civil engineer. Paul was the second of six children.

Paul Sereno (center) as Tom Sawyer in a school play

As a young boy, Paul didn't like school. Summer was his favorite season. He and his brothers and sisters would often sign up for nature classes. They went hiking. They collected leaves or insects. Soon they had an impressive insect collection and were hatching caterpillars in the house.

When he was in fourth grade, Paul went on his first fossil-hunting trip to an abandoned coal mine. Among the piles of rock, he found fossils of worms and other creatures that once lived at the bottom of an ancient sea. These fossils, older than dinosaur fossils, were pretty cool. But to Paul, a huge, beautifully colored moth, raised by hand from a tiny caterpillar—that was really cool!

Cecropia moth

One thing Paul did enjoy in school was art. In high school he created his first painting. It was a picture of bottles and the French horn he played in band. Paul decided he wanted to study art in college. But in order to get into college, he had to score well on the entrance exam. He devoted all his energies to this goal. He even read the dictionary during his lunch hour to learn new words.

The hard work paid off, and Paul was accepted at Northern Illinois University. There he took painting and other classes. Paul also studied **anatomy**, the structure of living things. He loved learning about how plants and animals have changed over millions of years.

The Turning Point

One fall while he was in college, Paul and his older brother visited the American Museum of Natural History in New York. On a behind-the-scenes tour, Paul saw the bones of strange creatures in room after room. He watched artists working on **reconstructions**, and he learned about scientists planning fossil-hunting trips to many parts of the world.

Though he loved art, Paul suddenly knew he wanted to be a **paleontologist**, a person who studies ancient life-forms. As a paleontologist, he could combine his talent in art with his interest in fossils and ancient life and his desire to explore the world. For Paul, paleontology seemed like the perfect job.

Paleontologists at the American Museum of Natural History clean the skull of a huge fossil reptile in the 1940s.

A year later, in 1979, Paul had a small desk among the fossils in the American Museum. He began studying paleontology at nearby Columbia University. It was an exciting time for paleontologists. Many students were trying to figure out family trees of different groups of animals and plants.

Despite their popularity, very little was known about dinosaurs. When and where did the first dinosaurs appear? How did dinosaurs evolve, or change over time? As he studied fossils, Paul's interest in dinosaurs grew. He wanted to answer these and other questions about these mysterious creatures.

After getting his doctoral degree at Columbia, Paul got a job teaching at the University of Chicago in 1987. That year he began planning his first expedition—to the Ischigualasto Valley in Argentina.

Word Power

The word *dinosaur* comes from the Greek words *deinos*, meaning "fearfully great," and *sauros*, meaning "lizard."

Discovering Dinosaurs

In the hot, dusty **badlands** of the Ischigualasto Valley, Paul and his team unearthed hundreds of fossils, including several partial skeletons of *Herrerasaurus*. Three years later, Paul returned to the valley to continue the work. This time the skeleton of a smaller dinosaur was discovered. Like *Herrerasaurus*, this meter-long (3-foot-long) cousin was a two-legged **carnivore**, or meat-eater. Unlike *Herrerasaurus*, this creature was a species that had never been found before, and it needed a name. Paul's team called it *Eoraptor*, which means "dawn stealer."

Skulls of *Eoraptor* reveal their small, razor-sharp teeth.

Paul Sereno and his team uncover an 18-meter (60-foot) dinosaur in Niger.

Next, Paul took a team to Africa. Their goal was to look for dinosaurs that lived when the mighty *Tyrannosaurus* roamed North America.

When *Eoraptor* lived—about 228 million years ago—all of the continents were joined in a single great **supercontinent** called Pangaea. By the last half of the dinosaur age, in the **Cretaceous** period (145–65 million years ago), Pangaea had broken apart into the continents we recognize today. The dinosaurs living on those continents became more and more different over time. So Paul knew that Africa's Cretaceous dinosaurs might look quite different from those in North America. When Paul set out for Africa, only a few dinosaurs had been discovered there. He began the search for dinosaur fossils in the Sahara, the world's largest desert. There among sand dunes and rocky cliffs, Paul and his team found many fossils, including some species new to science (see page 12).

You might wonder why Paul is so successful in his dinosaur detective work. After all, many paleontologists never find a new species. Paul says his success has to do with the kind of team that goes with him into the field. He takes students with a passion for fossils, young paleontologists, and sometimes a teacher, doctor, engineer, or photographer. They all share the dream of a major fossil discovery—and that takes them through all the hardships and challenges involved in working for months in a desert.

Interesting Questions

Q: Where can you find dinosaur fossils in the United States?

A: The western U.S. is considered one of the best fossil areas in the world. One bone-rich layer of rock extends more than 1,600 kilometers (1,000 miles) from New Mexico to Canada. Since 1877 when the first bones were discovered in this layer, many dinosaurs have been unearthed, including *Diplodocus, Apatosaurus, Allosaurus, Stegosaurus,* and *Brachiosaurus.*

Afrovenator
New species discovered in Niger. It was 9 meters (30 feet) long, with long, pointed teeth.

Jobaria
New species discovered in Niger. This huge **herbivore**, or plant-eater, grew to more than 18 meters (60 feet) in length.

Deltadromeus
New species discovered in Morocco. With its long, slender legs, *Deltadromeus* must have been the track star of the dinosaur world 90 million years ago.

Carcharodontosaurus
Discovered in Morocco, it's among the largest carnivores that ever roamed Earth, with a nearly 2-meter-long (6-foot-long) skull.

That Crocodile Smile

One of the new species that Paul and his team discovered in Africa was especially strange-looking. The clue that led to its discovery was a giant thumb claw that was just lying on the surface of the desert as if someone had put it there yesterday. Actually, it was about 100 million years old! After digging around the claw, the team unearthed most of a huge skeleton that was 11 meters (36 feet) long. Like *Tyrannosaurus*, it was a **predator**. But this dinosaur had a sail on its back and a long, low skull with more than a hundred teeth in its jaws. Paul's team named it *Suchomimus*, meaning "crocodile mimic," because its skull looked a bit like a crocodile's.

Suchomimus's teeth were sharp, and the largest ones were located at the front of the jaws. Paleontologists often **infer** what dinosaurs ate by the shape of their fossilized teeth. To infer means to draw a conclusion based on what you know. Paul and his team inferred that *Suchomimus* might have snapped up **prey** as a crocodile does, because its teeth are similar to a crocodile's.

After making so many discoveries in Africa, Paul's reputation as a dinosaur hunter spread. Many people wanted to hunt for fossils with Paul. Have you ever wondered what it would be like to hunt for dinosaur fossils? Well, grab your hat and sunscreen and let's join Paul on one of his recent expeditions.

Paul shows the teeth of *Suchomimus*.

CHAPTER TWO

In the Field
Digging Up Dinosaurs

You are in dinosaur territory—on the southern edge of the Sahara in the country of Niger in West Africa. It's 10 a.m. on an autumn day and it's already 50°C (120°F). Your mouth is dry and lips are cracked, but you don't notice. You're on your knees, hunched over a dinosaur skull. That's all that matters.

This tooth belongs to the *Carcharodontosaurus,* a predator that lived 90 million years ago.

With a paintbrush you gently sweep away sand and pebbles from some of the pointed teeth in the dinosaur's lower jaw. Slowly, more of the skull emerges, and the glinting teeth almost look like the dinosaur is smiling back at you for the expert dental work you've done! Nearby, Paul and some team members are uncovering the fossils of other kinds of dinosaurs. You stop to stretch, take a drink of water, and get a quick update on their finds.

For Paul and his team, finding fossils involves spending long and tiring hours working beneath the scorching sun. There can be many false clues—a stone that looks like a bone, a bone fragment that doesn't lead anywhere.

Paul brushes a huge thigh bone of *Jobaria* in the Sahara.

You've heard Paul and the other team members say that the complete skeletons are rare and often have only a few edges exposed at the surface. That's why they are still complete—because most of the bone is protected by rock. That's also what makes them difficult to find. And to dig up!

Your break is over—back to work. You hope to have most of the dinosaur's smile exposed by the end of the day. By then you'll be tired and really hungry. As drops of sweat drip off your face, you think about how nice it will be to get something to eat and relax under the stars back at camp.

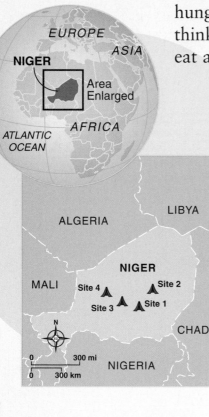

Trucks carry supplies from one campsite to another.

A Desert Camp

Team members pack up the campsite.

Over the past weeks you've camped in four different places on this Niger expedition. What does a team of 14 dinosaur hunters need to create a temporary home in the desert? Water—lots of it—and more than a ton of food. There's a big first-aid kit and 4.5 kilograms (10 pounds) of sunscreen. Lots of tools and equipment are necessary. Each person has a tent, sleeping bag, and cot. Larger tents serve as the kitchen, a storage shed, and a place to work on fossils. The team uses trucks to get around. Large trucks move the team and the camp to new locations. They also transport heavy loads of fossils at the end of the fieldwork.

Fragile Treasures

The desert sun is sinking toward the western horizon. You've made good progress. Paul says your dinosaur skull is exposed enough to remove it from the ground tomorrow. But you've learned that's not a simple job.

The skull has survived more than 100 million years only because it was embedded in rock. If you try to lift it out of the ground, it will break into pieces.

Suchomimus fossils are wrapped with cloth soaked in plaster for protection during transport.

So you must dig around the bones and wrap them with the surrounding rock in a plaster "hard case." That will make it possible to transport them safely out of the desert.

How do you build this hard case around a dinosaur fossil? You use big strips of burlap cloth, which have been soaked in wet **plaster**. The plaster-soaked cloth is carefully wrapped around the block of fossil and rock. In the desert air, the plaster dries quickly to form a rock-hard jacket. Safe inside this hard shell, the fossil is ready to be moved.

Members of the team load plaster-wrapped fossils into a truck.

In their hard jackets, some of the fossils you've collected on this expedition weigh more than a ton. They are lifted onto the back of a truck using a giant tripod and pulleys. As Paul's team travels across the desert, this precious cargo is loaded and unloaded several times—first at a central point in the field and then at a nearby oasis. Eventually, the fossils will be transported by truck to Ghana on the coast of Africa.

Tools of the Trade

Paleontologist Paul Sereno and his teams use many different kinds of tools on fossil-hunting expeditions.

▶ COMPASS – A compass helps paleontologists determine the direction in which they need to travel.

▼ MAPS – Paleontologists use maps to locate rock types and features of the landscape such as rivers and mountains. Paleontologists also make detailed maps of a site where fossils are found. These maps show exactly how each bone or skeleton is positioned in or on the ground.

▶ AWL – This is a paleontologist's most important tool. It is useful for digging, probing, scratching, and loosening rock from around delicate fossils.

▼ PICK – Team members use this tool to quickly remove sand and rock when they are not working too close to dinosaur bones.

▼ DENTAL INSTRUMENTS – These tools are used for very detailed work, such as digging up tiny bits of bone and cleaning rock off dinosaur teeth that are millions of years old.

Don't Leave
Home
Without It!

Many Africans living in and around the Sahara wear good luck charms called *gris-gris* (gree-gree). The charms are little sacks made of camel leather. They are filled with herbs and other small objects thought to protect a person from danger. Paul and most of his team members quickly picked up on the habit.

▼ CAMERA – Paleontologists take pictures of every step of a dinosaur excavation. Photographs are helpful when it's time to put bones back together. Photographs help scientists remember how the bones were found lying together in the ground.

▲ BRUSHES – The team uses these tools to carefully remove sand and pebbles from around buried bones.

CHAPTER THREE

Bringing Bones to Life
Rebuilding Dinosaurs

So 20 tons of dinosaur fossils have been shipped from Africa to the United States. What happens to those fossils? What can Paul Sereno and his team learn from them?

When jacketed dinosaur fossils arrive at Paul's lab, they are organized in a storage area. Then they are opened, carefully, one at a time. The jacket is placed on a table. One side of the jacket is opened, and the exposed side of the fossils is carefully cleaned. The fragile cracks are hardened with glue. A base is made to support that side of the fossil, and the fossil is turned to rest on that base. Now the other half of the jacket is removed and that side of the fossil is cleaned.

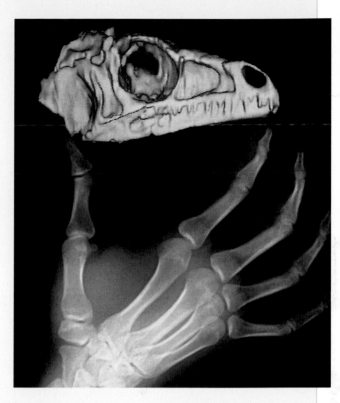

This CT scan shows an *Eoraptor* skull.

Once this is done, Paul and other paleontologists can examine the fossils very closely. They make drawings and take photographs.

Paleontologists often use microscopes to look at the details of bones or teeth. They also use **CT scans**. With a CT scan, experts can see inside bones. A CT scan is made from x-rays that penetrate a fossil to show internal details, such as hidden teeth inside jaws or the space for the brain inside the skull.

Back in the lab, fossils are carefully cleaned after the plaster jacket is removed.

Many of the dinosaur fossils Paul and his teams find are newly discovered species, so each and every bone is important. Scientists look at the teeth and search for signs of wear and tear. Researchers study the size and shape of the bones and how the bones worked together. They also compare the bones to those of other dinosaurs. Similarities in the bones of different kinds of dinosaurs can show how closely those dinosaurs are related. This information can help researchers figure out the details of the dinosaur family tree and how dinosaurs evolved.

Building a Dinosaur

The last step is to put the fossils together as a skeleton. A skeleton shows the shape of the dinosaur. But fossils are heavy and fragile. That's because in the process of fossilization, all of the small spaces in a bone get filled in with rock. After fossilization, dozens of cracks form around these rock-filled spaces. Instead of using these delicate fossils, a **cast,** or exact copy, of the fossils is used to build a skeleton for display. Unless you're an expert, it's hard to tell a cast of a fossil from the real thing. A cast also can be used by other scientists who want to study the specimen.

Paul Sereno stands between skeletons of an adult and young *Jobaria* in the courtyard of the National Geographic Society. These skeletons are casts of the original fossils.

When all the bones are cast, a dinosaur skeleton can at last be pieced together on a steel frame. Using information gathered from studying the bones, Paul designs a life-like pose for the skeleton. A team in a metal-working shop makes the steel frame and attaches the bone casts.

With its back arched and toothy mouth open as if in a snarl, it's easy to imagine a dinosaur suddenly stepping out of a display and going in search of a meal!

Art and Science

As a scientist, Paul Sereno knows that fossil bones and teeth can tell only so much about how a dinosaur looked when it was alive. We don't really know, for example, if dinosaurs had spots or stripes, or if they were dull or brightly colored.

As an artist, Paul knows that a little creativity can go a long way in making dinosaurs come alive. He often works with dinosaur artists who create drawings, paintings, and sculptures of dinosaurs as they *might* have looked in the flesh. These artists take what Paul has learned from studying dinosaur bones and combine that information with what they know about muscles, organs, and skin in living animals. Then they season all that with a good dash of imagination. In this way, science and art come together to give us a new look at dinosaurs. To add to that remarkable view, paleontologist Paul Sereno plans to keep on looking for dinosaur fossils in far-flung corners of the world.

This illustration shows a large *Carcharodontosaurus* protecting its meal from the smaller *Deltadromeus*.

A hundred teeth and thumb claws like daggers? *Suchomimus* must have been one cool beast! Perhaps you want to know more about this dinosaur. Where's the best place to look? The steps below can help you choose the best sources for dependable answers to your questions about *Suchomimus*, or any other topic.

STEP 1 Identify a Wide Variety of Possible Resources

At your school or public library you can find many sources of information such as books, magazines, newspapers, and videos about *Suchomimus* or other dinosaurs. You might also search for information on the Internet. An interview with a fossil expert or museum employee might turn out to be a gold mine.

STEP 2 Evaluate and Choose the Best Sources

The next step is deciding which sources are best for your needs. Getting current information is important. So eliminate sources that are out-of-date. Also pick reliable sources that will contain factual information.

Which do you think are more reliable sources?
- A book written by Paul Sereno about his discoveries OR a science-fiction video about cloned dinosaurs brought to life in the modern world
- A website sponsored by a society of paleontologists OR one selling dinosaur T-shirts

STEP 3 Locate Information

After selecting the best sources, you need to find the information that will help answer your questions.

If your source is a book:
- Scan the table of contents. It gives a quick overview of the various topics in the book.
- Turn to the index and check to see if your topic is listed.

When searching websites:
- Click on the site map. It shows where certain kinds of information can be found.
- Type your topic into the SEARCH box. It can take you directly to Web pages on your topic.

STEP 4 Follow Leads to Other Sources

Each source you investigate may lead to other sources.
- Look for a bibliography that lists other books or articles on the same topic.
- Links in one website lead to other sites.
- A person you interview may suggest other people to talk to, or an information source you hadn't considered.

Did you know that . . .

. . . during the day, dinosaur bones exposed to the sun in the Sahara can reach a temperature of 65°C (150°F)—almost hot enough to fry an egg?

. . . on Paul Sereno's expedition to Niger in 2000, the team used 100 hundred-pound bags of plaster to make jackets around the fossils they shipped back to the U.S.?

. . . it's possible to have ice cream bars for dessert on Paul's desert expeditions? Freeze-dried, of course.

Books to Read

Dingus, Lowell. *Next of Kin: Great Fossils at the American Museum of Natural History.* Rizzoli, 1996.

Gaffney, Eugene S. *Dinosaurs.* St. Martin Press, 2001.

Haines, Tim. *Walking with Dinosaurs: A Natural History.* DK Publishing, 2000.

Sereno, Paul. *How Tough Was a Tyrannosaurus? More Fascinating Facts About Dinosaurs.* Price Stern Sloan, 1989.

Websites to Visit

www.nationalgeographic.com/ dinoquest

www.projectexploration.org

dinosaur.uchicago.edu

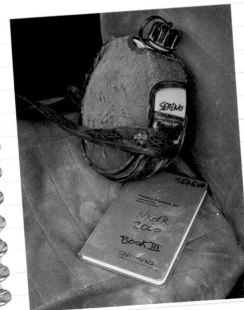

Glossary

anatomy – the study of the structure of living things

badland – a dry region marked by small, steep hills, deep gullies, and few plants

carnivore – an animal that eats the flesh of other animals

cast – an exact copy of a fossil

Cretaceous *(kree-TAY-shuhs)* – the period in Earth's history between 145 and 65 million years ago

CT scan – a special kind of x-ray that allows scientists to see inside bones

evolve – to change over time

extinct – no longer living

fossil – the remains or mark left by a plant or animal that lived long ago

herbivore – a plant-eating animal

infer – to draw a conclusion based on what you know

paleontologist *(pay-lee-ahn-TAHL-uh-jist)* – a scientist who studies fossils of plants and animals that lived long ago

plaster – a thick, sticky mixture generally made from lime, sand, and water that hardens when it dries

predator – an animal that captures and eats other animals

prey – an animal that is eaten by another animal

reconstruction – a model made to show what something once looked like

species – a subgroup in the classification plan of living things

supercontinent – one large continent made up of all the present continents before they split apart and drifted to their present locations

Index